KS1 Science Revision Guide

Jackie Clegg

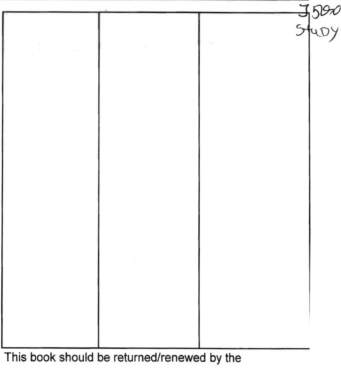

Welcom
Whimst
scientifi

Whimst
you. He

Pointy –

And Mugly and Bugly – Pointy's lazy
pet frogs, who prefer eating and
snoozing to learning, but still have a
few tricks to teach

Just work your way through the pages of th
too will become a real Science wizard like W
and his friends!

Good luck, young wizard!

Contents

⭐ My Body

tick when complete

⭐ In the Garden

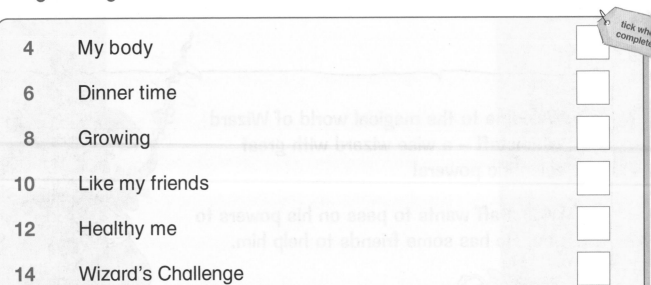

Magical Materials

My World

My body

> We are going to look at the different parts of our body, young wizard.

⭐ Body bits!

All humans have similar bodies. Can you name all of the parts of your body? Look at this picture of me.

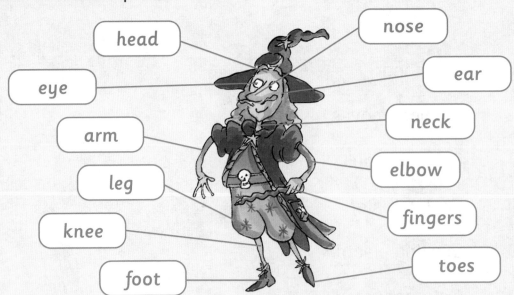

head

eye

arm

leg

knee

foot

nose

ear

neck

elbow

fingers

toes

My friends Miss Snufflebeam and Mugly and Bugly have different kinds of bodies.

Allakazan! A lot of their body parts have the same names as ours. Look at the picture of Miss Snufflebeam. Can you point to these body parts? Head, finger, nose, neck and leg.

Have you noticed that on our body we have two of everything down the sides and one of everything in the middle?

My senses.

Let me tell you about our wonderful senses.

Sit very still and listen to what is going on around you. What can you hear? Hearing is one of our senses.

These are the five things senses can do:

see   hear   smell   touch   taste

We use different parts of our body for each of the different senses.

seeing   hearing   smelling   touching   tasting

 Have you noticed that most of our senses come from our head?

Wizard's Practice

Workbook pages 4-5

Now have a go at writing down which sense matches each of these body parts. Hey presto!

1 nose _____

2 finger _____

3 eye _____

4 tongue _____

5 ear _____

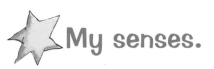

Dinner time

Slurp! We all need to eat and drink to stay alive. We like to eat bugs! What do you like to eat?

We need to eat!

Burp! These are some of the things that we like to eat!

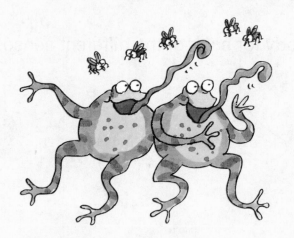

Different animals eat different things. Look at the animals with the food they like to eat below. Grub's up! Time for a snack…

Healthy diet.

Slurp! It is important to eat different types of food. We can put foods into groups together.

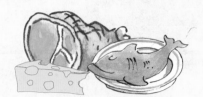

Croak! You should eat some food from each group. This is a **healthy diet**.

It is not good for your body to eat too many foods from one group. If someone only eats chips, they might become fat and feel tired all the time! This would be an **unhealthy diet**. We also need to drink lots of water and so do you!

 Eating '5 a day' of fresh fruit and vegetables keeps us healthy.

MAGIC WORDS   healthy • diet • unhealthy

Workbook pages 6-7

Wizard's Practice

Write the word **Healthy** or **Unhealthy** at the end of each menu.

1 fried fish and chips _____

2 cheese salad and an apple _____

3 a packet of crisps and a chocolate bar _____

4 pasta with ham and tomato _____

5 fried bacon, sausage and eggs _____

Growing

I started life as an egg, but not everyone starts their life this way! Wizard Whimstaff says that humans start their lives as babies.

⭐ **Growing up!**

Abracadada! As I **grow**, I change. Do you look the same now as when you were a baby? Look at these pictures of me.

The pictures below show some of my friends with their mums.

Cabradababa! As I grew, I became **taller**. So did you!

Changes

Growing up is more than just getting taller.
I also become **heavier** as I grow.

Other changes take place as we grow. Girls become more shapely as they become women. Some men grow beards.

Mugly and Bugly had lots of changes as they grew up from tadpoles.

A butterfly also goes through lots of changes. It starts off as an egg, which hatches into a caterpillar. Next, it turns into a chrysalis and finally changes into a butterfly.

Human babies and some animal babies have to be looked after by their parents.

MAGIC WORDS   grow • taller • heavier

Workbook pages 8-9

Wizard's Practice

Can you help me? Draw lines to match these babies with their parents.

1 puppy	hen
2 chick	butterfly
3 caterpillar	dog
4 kitten	frog
5 tadpole	cat

Like my friends

Look around you. Your classmates and family look similar to you. Super!

⭐ Humans

Humans (and goblins) are born with two eyes, two ears, two arms and two legs.

Humans have **similar** bodies to each other.

We all have hair, but we choose to have different hair styles!

All birds have wings and a beak.

All fish have fins and a tail.

Investigating differences.

We look like our friends, but we all have some differences.

My hair is a different colour from Wizard Whimstaff's hair.

My nose is a different shape.

Wizard Whimstaff is taller than me.

Wizard Whimstaff is older than me.

We did an investigation to see if older people are always taller than younger people. We measured the **height** of 5 children.

Here are our results.

We found out that older children are usually taller than younger children, but not always.

age in years	height in cm
2	80
4	124
6	150
8	145
10	182

 Look for other similarities like eye colour, hair colour and size of feet.

 MAGIC WORDS | humans • similar • different • height

Wizard's Practice

Workbook pages 10-11

Now write **T** for True or **F** for False next to each sentence, thinking about your own classmates.

1. All children in my class have blue eyes. _____

2. All children in my class have two ears. _____

3. All children in my class have a nose. _____

4. All children in my class have black hair. _____

5. All children in my class wear size 3 shoes. _____

Healthy me

Can you help me? I want to be healthy, but I am not sure what to do. I like to **exercise**, but sometimes it makes me feel tired!

⭐ Feeling good!

Look at Pointy. He is getting hot and thirsty. Do you feel hot and thirsty after exercise? Make sure that you drink plenty of water!

Abracadada! Exercise keeps you healthy and makes you feel good. There are lots of different things you can do.

Mugly and Bugly like to swim.

Pointy and I like to play football.

Pointy likes to ride his bike.

What is your favourite type of exercise?

Feeling bad.

Oh dear! Sometimes we get ill. Pointy is feeling sick.

Dabracababa! The doctor will give Pointy some **medicine** to make him feel better.

We cannot take Pointy's medicine. It could make us ill. You must only take medicine when a grown up gives it to you.

Always follow these three rules to keep you safe:

1 Do not take more medicine than you have been told to.

2 Be careful, because tablets can look like sweets.

3 Never take anything from the medicine cupboard.

We should not eat anything unless we know what it is.

 MAGIC WORDS exercise • medicine

Wizard's Practice

Workbook pages 12-13

Can you help me to fill in the missing words? Choose your words from this list:

> exercise   healthy   hot   medicine   sweets

1 To stay healthy, we need to _____.

2 When you exercise, you become tired and _____.

3 When we are ill, a doctor gives us _____.

4 The medicine will help us to feel _____ again.

5 We need to be careful, because some pills look like _____.

Wizard's Challenge

 My body!

Slurp! Different parts of your body are for different senses. Match the body part to its correct sense.

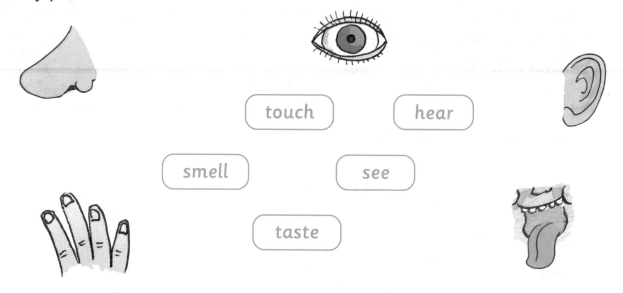

touch   hear

smell   see

taste

 Dinner time!

Burp! You should have 5 servings a day of fruit and vegetables. We prefer flies!

a Circle the '5 a day', while we go for a snack.

b Fill in the missing words. Choose them from this list.

diet   exercise   group   pop   water

For a healthy _____, you should have a small amount from

each food _____ and drink plenty of _____.

3 Growing!

These pictures show us growing up.
Put the letters into the correct order.

b				

We have done the first one for you.

a

b
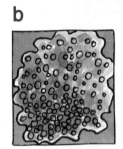

c
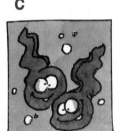

d

e

4 Like my friends.

Miss Snufflebeam looked at the eye colour of all the children in her class.

Pointy drew a bar chart of her results.

Croak! Look at the bar chart and try to answer the questions.

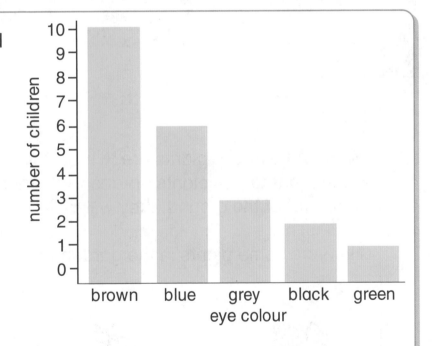

a How many children have brown eyes? _____

b How many children have black eyes? _____

c 6 children have _____ coloured eyes.

d Only one child has _____ coloured eyes.

Plants

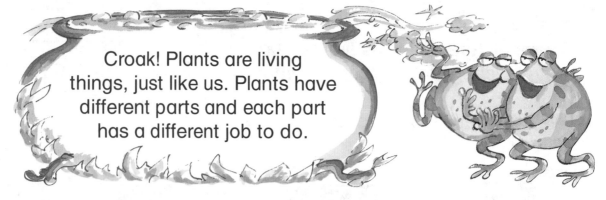

Croak! Plants are living things, just like us. Plants have different parts and each part has a different job to do.

★ Plants in the garden.

There are lots of plants in our garden. They are all very different. Have you seen any of these plants?

a tree   grass   daisy   pondweed

Slurp! All of these plants are **living**. Pointy says that we must be very careful not to pull plants up and that we must look after them. If we pull them out of the ground, they will die!

Here are some plants in the garden that provide you with food.

lettuce   carrot   celery   apple

These foods are good for you and are part of your '5 a day'!

⭐ Plant parts.

Plants have different parts. Do you know what each part is for?

flower		leaf
stem		roots

	attracts insects		hold plant in the ground and take in water
	makes food for the plant		carries food and water to all parts of the plant

 Roots are not green. Only the parts of the plant that are in sunlight are green.

MAGIC WORDS   living • flower • leaf • stem • roots

Wizard's Practice

Workbook pages 14-15

Burp! Draw five lines to match the part of the plant with the job that it does. One part does two jobs!

☆1 flower   carries food and water around the plant

☆2 leaf   keep the plant in the soil

☆3 roots   where food is made for the plant

☆4 roots   suck up water from the soil

☆5 stem   attracts insects to visit the plant

Plants can grow

Let me tell you about what plants need to grow.

⭐ **Plants need water.**

Hey presto! Plants need **water** to live, just like you do! Without water, plants will turn brown and dry.

with water   without water

The roots suck water up from the soil. Look at the picture to see how water travels through the plant when Pointy waters it.

Plants need light.

Pointy and I put a box over a plant. Then we went off to do some spells and we forgot all about it.

Two weeks later we took the box off.
The plant had gone yellow!

This is because plants need **sunlight** to live.

With sunlight and water, plants have healthy growth.

As they grow, they get taller.

As they grow taller, they grow more leaves. Allakazan!

 Plants need water and sunlight to stay healthy and to grow.

 MAGIC WORDS water • sunlight

 Workbook pages 16-17

Wizard's Practice

Circle the correct word for each sentence.

1 One of the things plants need to live is **soil / sweets / water.**

2 Another thing plants need to grow is **sunlight / music / quiet.**

3 Plants without water turn **yellow / green / brown.**

4 Plants without light turn **yellow / green / brown.**

5 As plants grow, they become taller and grow more *flies / leaves / hairs.*

Where plants and animals live

Nothing seems to live inside Wizard Whimstaff's cave, but lots of things live in the gardens. I wonder why?

★ What lives here?

Look at the picture of Wizard Whimstaff's cave. Can you see any plants or animals living here?

Oh yes! A spider. Not much else.

Dabracababa! Look at the picture of a field. Can you see anything living here?

There are lots of **plants** growing here. Can you see animals as well? Pointy says that the **animals** are here because they have plants to eat and live on. They also have water to drink and play in.

Would you expect to see these animals in a field?

No, because these animals live in different places!

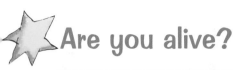

Are you alive?

Oh dear! I am confused.
Pointy says that my toy dragon is not alive.

Pointy says that we are living because
we can do all of these things:

feed

move

breathe

feel things

grow

have babies

get rid of waste

Now I understand. My toy dragon can move, but it cannot do all of these things. So my toy dragon is not alive.

 Plants are living, so they do all of these things.

MAGIC WORDS — plants • animals

Wizard's Practice

Workbook pages 18-19

Can you help me? Write **T** for True or **F** for False next to each sentence.

1. My toy dragon can move, so it is a living thing. _____

2. Plants can do all 7 of these things, so they are living. _____

3. Wizard Whimstaff's car moves, gets rid of waste and feeds, so it is living. _____

4. Mugly and Bugly can do all 7 of these things, so they are living. _____

5. You can do all 7 of these things, but you are not living. _____

Seeds

When **seeds** sprout, and start to grow, it seems like magic! It's easy when you know how!

Seeds from plants.

Look at all these seeds.

Seeds come from the flower of a plant. As seeds start to grow, the flower dies. The seeds grow until they are ready to be planted.

Some seeds are found inside **fruits**. Look at these pictures. Can you see the seeds?

What seeds need to sprout!

We can get new plants from seeds. Super! When the seed is ready to **sprout**, the case around the seed splits open. Then the new young plant can start to grow.

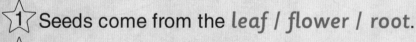

I am **investigating** to find out what seeds need to sprout. I have put seeds onto cotton wool. The pictures show what I will do with the dishes.

this dish has water   this dish has no water

Here are my results.

From my investigation I have shown that seeds need water to sprout.

 Seeds can sprout on lots of different materials. They do not need soil to sprout.

MAGIC WORDS   seeds • fruits • sprout • investigating

Wizard's Practice

Workbook pages 20-21

Circle the correct word for each sentence. Practice makes perfect!

1. Seeds come from the *leaf / flower / root*.

2. The outer case splits open when the seed is ready to *grow / die / sprout*.

3. Seeds can be found inside some *fruits / leaves / roots*.

4. For seeds to sprout they need warmth and *light / cold / water*.

5. New plants can sprout from *seeds / roots / water*.

Into groups

Slurp! Sometimes you will need to sort things into different groups. We always put things into two groups, things we can eat and things we cannot eat!

Living and non-living.

Can you remember what living things do?
Look at page 21 to remind yourself.

We sorted these things into **non-living** and **living**.

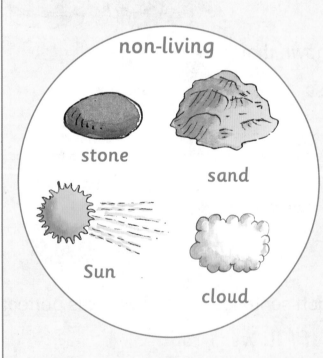

non-living

stone

sand

Sun

cloud

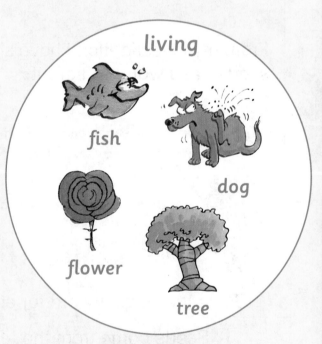

living

fish

dog

flower

tree

We are living. We know we are alive because we need feeding!
Time for a snack!

Plants and animals.

Burp! We are trying to group the living things in our garden.
We will group them as **animals** or **plants**.

animals

plants

We can group the animals again.
We shall group them into animals with legs and animals with no legs.

animals with legs

animals with no legs

Croak! You can group things by what is similar and by what is different.
Is it time for a snooze yet? Zzzz…

 Humans are part of the animal group.

MAGIC WORDS living • non-living • animals • plants

Workbook pages 22-23

Wizard's Practice

Draw five lines to match each description to the correct thing.

1 non-living   tree

2 plant with thick trunk   sand

3 plant with flowers   slug

4 animal with no legs   cat

5 animal with legs   rose

Wizard's Challenge

1 Plants

Slurp! Can you label this diagram for us? Use these words to help you:

flower   leaf   stem   roots

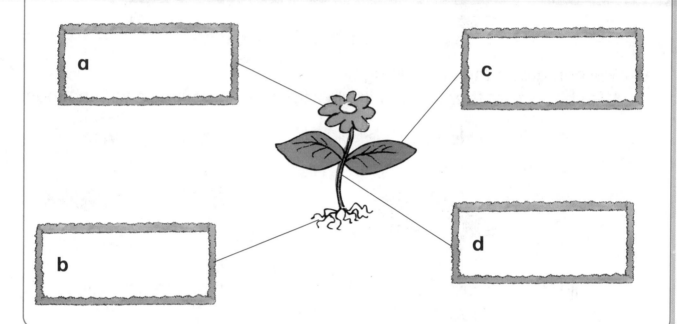

a

c

b

d

2 Plants can grow.

Croak! Draw a line to match the plant with the correct description.

light and water   no water   no light

3 Where plants and animals live.

Burp! Match each animal to the picture of where they live, by drawing a line. We have done the first one for you. Complete the rest while we have a snooze.

4 Seeds

a We want to grow some plants. Pointy has given us seeds and instructions, but we have mixed up the instructions. Can you help us to sort them out? Pointy has done the first one for you.

Water the seeds regularly. ☐   Collect some soil in a pot. 1

Plant the seeds in the soil. ☐   Place the pot in a warm place. ☐

Now finish the sentences by writing in the missing words.

grow   sprout   seeds

b We can get new plants from _____ .

c When the seed is ready to _____, the case splits open.

d Then the new young plant can start to _____ .

Materials

Now we are going to look at materials, young wizard. All objects are made up of materials. Allakazan!

⭐ Properties

Let me tell you about **materials**. Here are some materials.

stone

metal

glass

fabric

These materials have different **properties**. The stone is hard, the metal is shiny, the glass is transparent and the fabric is soft.

Hard, soft, transparent and shiny are all properties. All of these materials are solids.

Liquids and gases are also materials.

Liquids can flow.
Air fills its container.

water

air

Matching materials!

Now we are going to see how important properties are. The properties of a material are matched to its use.

This pillow is made from feathers, because they are soft.

This chair is made of wood, because it is strong.

This window is made of glass, because it is transparent.

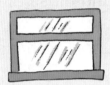

It would not be a good idea to make a bed out of stone!

MAGIC WORDS   materials • properties

Workbook pages 24-25

Wizard's Practice

Hey presto! Now try these. Circle the correct property for each of the materials.

1. metal   flows / shiny / transparent
2. glass   flows / soft / transparent
3. water   flows / shiny / transparent
4. wool   soft / hard / flows
5. stone   soft / hard / flows

Sorting

Pointy says that some materials can be found in nature. I thought that people made materials!

⭐ Natural and manufactured.

Some materials like stone, wood and straw can be found in nature. Abracadada! We call these **natural materials**. Materials like plastic and glass are made by people. We call these **manufactured** materials.

Look at these materials. I have sorted them into two groups.

natural materials

manufactured materials

Pointy says that people can use natural materials to make objects.

sheep → wool   wood → chair   clay → cup   stone → paving slab

Magnetic metals.

Pointy gave me a magnet. He said some of my things will be attracted to the magnet and some will not.

I tested my things with the magnet. I **predicted** that the metal things will be **magnetic** and the non-metal things will not.

magnetic   non-magnetic

Oh dear! My prediction was not quite right. My metal car is magnetic but my train is not.

Pointy says that only some metals are magnetic, but materials that are not metal cannot be magnetic.

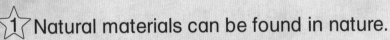

MAGIC WORDS natural materials • manufactured • predict • magnetic

Workbook pages 26-27

Wizard's Practice

Can you help me? Write **T** for True and **F** for False next to each sentence.

1. Natural materials can be found in nature. _____
2. All metals are magnetic. _____
3. All non-metals are non-magnetic. _____
4. Wool is a natural material. _____
5. Plastic is a natural material. _____

Changing

Croak! Materials can be changed by doing different things to them.

Changing shape.

Slurp! We like to play in clay. The clay is like play dough. You can make lots of fun things out of it. I like to squash it and bend it. Bugly likes to stretch it and twist it.

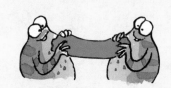

We cannot do this with stones. They will not change.

Heating up!

Burp! Mugly has made a cup out of clay. We will heat it in the oven. The clay changes and becomes hard.

Pointy says that other materials change when we heat them up. This happens when we cook our food. Time for a snack!

This change is simpler. The **solid** is turning into a **liquid**.

Croak! We can cool this down again and turn it back into ice. The liquid turns back into a solid.

 When a solid turns into a liquid, we call this melting.

Cooling down.

Burp! In winter, the surface of our pond **freezes**.

When the Sun comes out, it gets warmer and the ice **melts**. This is a useful change.

Pointy has left the kettle on in the kitchen.

As the water boils, steam comes out of the top. This is a liquid turning into a **gas**.

The steam hits the window and turns back into water.

We like water! Slurp!

When a liquid turns into a solid, we call this freezing.

  solid • liquid • freezes • melts • gas

Wizard's Practice

Workbook pages 28-29

Which of these materials will change when you heat them up? Write **Y** for Yes and **N** for No.

 1 ice cube   _____

2 paper cup   _____

 3 stone   _____

4 cheese   _____

 5 egg   _____

Wizard's Challenge

 Materials

Croak! Choose the best material to make each of these objects.
Write the type of material below each object.

| glass   metal   plastic   wood |

a

b

c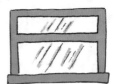

d

_____   _____   _____   _____

 Properties

Burp! Draw a line to match each picture of a property to its description.

(keeps its shape)   (can flow easily)   (can fill its container)

3 Sorting

Slurp! Some things are found in nature and some things are made by people. Draw a circle around the things that are made by people.

4 Metals

Here are some sentences about metals. Write in the missing words.

magnetic   metals   non-metals

a Some _____ are shiny.

b Not all metals are _____ .

c All _____ are non-magnetic.

5 Water, steam and ice.

Here are some sentences about changes. Write in the missing words. Choose your word from the list below.

steam   ice   water

a When it gets very cold, water changes into _____ .

b When steam cools, it changes into _____ .

c When water gets very hot, it changes into _____ .

I can see

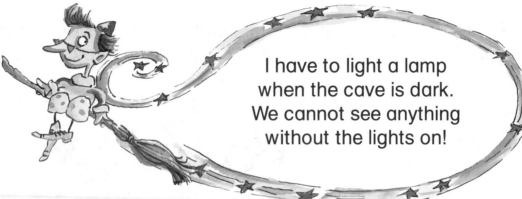

I have to light a lamp when the cave is dark. We cannot see anything without the lights on!

 **In the dark!**

Our cave is very **dark**. When I light a candle, then I can see things. The candle gives out light, so we call it a **light source**. Can you see other light sources in our cave?

The candle, the fire and the torch are all light sources. Super!

Other light sources are:

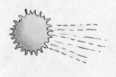   

Sun   lamp   fireworks   TV   computer

We see things because the light shines on them.
It's easy when you know how!

Shiny things!

Miss Snufflebeam is confused. She thought that light came from a mirror.

The mirror is not a light source. It **reflects** light.

Light from a light source, such as a lamp, bounces off the mirror. **Shiny** things reflect light very well.

The Sun is a strong light source. You must never look directly at the Sun, as it is very bright and could burn your eyes.

MAGIC WORDS dark • light source • reflects • shiny

Wizard's Practice

Workbook pages 30-31

Practice makes perfect! Write **S** next to a light source or **R** next to an object that reflects light.

1. mirror _____
2. candle _____
3. torch _____
4. glitter _____
5. Sun _____

Silly sounds

Oh dear! Sometimes I hear sounds and they scare me! Help me to find out what makes sound.

⭐ Making sounds.

Listen carefully. What can you hear? Can you hear sounds outside the room?

Lots of different things make sounds.

All of these sounds are **loud**. If you listen more carefully, can you hear other sounds? Look at these pictures.

These things all make **quiet** sounds.

Music or noise?

Can you make a loud sound? Look at these different ways of making sounds.

Oh dear! They are making a noise. Pointy says that noise is unwanted sound.

Music is a much nicer sound. You can dance to music! Can you make music too?

Some musical instruments make a **low** sound.

Some musical instruments make a **high** sound.

Sounds are made when things move.

 Put your fingers on your throat and you can feel your voice box moving when you sing!

 loud • quiet • low • high

Workbook pages 32-33

Wizard's Practice

Write **L** for Loud or **Q** for Quiet next to these sounds.

1 dog barking   _____

2 grass moving in breeze   _____

3 children shouting   _____

4 fire engine   _____

5 clock ticking   _____

I can hear

We use our ears to listen to lots of things. Allakazan! You can use your ears to work out where a sound is coming from.

⭐ My ears!

Your ears can hear sounds. Close your eyes and **listen** carefully. Hey presto! Can you hear any sounds? Now point to where it is coming from.

Sound travels through the air. Sounds then go into our ears and we can hear the sound.

Some people work in noisy places. They need to protect their ears. Loud **noise** can damage your ears

Some children listen to music whilst riding their bike. This is dangerous. The children cannot hear the cars around them.

Sounds can warn you of danger. So it is important to use your ears, especially when you are on the road!

Don't play games near to the road, because it will distract you from listening to what is happening around you.

Can you hear it?

I like to listen to music on the radio. Do you like music?

I move away from the radio. I can still **hear** the music, but it is not as **loud**.

I go into another room. I can still hear the music, but it is very **quiet** now.

Do you play your music loudly or quietly? Miss Snufflebeam plays her nursery rhymes softly, but Mugly and Bugly like to sing along to loud pop music!

You cannot see sound travelling through the air.

MAGIC WORDS listen• noise • hear • loud • quiet

Wizard's Practice

Workbook pages 34-35

Finish these sentences by writing in the missing word. Choose your words from this list:

> ears   loud   danger   quieter   travels

1. We hear sounds with our _____.

2. Sound _____ through the air.

3. Sounds can warn us of _____.

4. Your ears can be damaged by _____ sounds.

5. The further away you are from the radio, the

   _____ the sound.

Magical moves

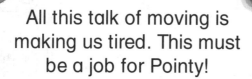

All this talk of moving is making us tired. This must be a job for Pointy!

⭐ On the move!

Croak! Look at the pictures. Some things stay still. Some things can **move**. Can you work out which things can move?

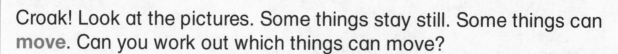

Pointy went for a walk in the park. He saw lots of different ways of moving. Do you do some of these things?

Slurp! There are lots of different ways to move:

Sliding.

Turning.

Swinging.

Moving up and down.

Take care!

Moving objects can be dangerous. Take care when crossing the road. Moving cars are **heavy**. They will push you over and hurt you.

Cars can move fast, so it can take them a long time to stop.

Always look carefully before you cross the road.

Take care! There are other moving objects that could hurt you.

MAGIC WORDS move • heavy

Wizard's Practice

Workbook pages 36-37

Burp! Tick the sentences that describe something moving.

1 My house is made of brick. ☐

2 The train is travelling fast. ☐

3 The statue is very tall. ☐

4 The children are playing football. ☐

5 The bus is coming. ☐

43

Push and pull

Pulling and pushing can be lots of fun, but we must always be careful not to pull or push too hard! Abracababa!

 ## Pushing and pulling!

Pointy says we use **pushes** and **pulls** everyday. Here are some pushes that you do! Pushing things starts them moving.

Here are some pulls. These pulls are making things move.

Here are some more pushes and pulls. Which ones do you do?

pull   push and pull   push

 Sometimes a push or a pull can stop an object moving.

Squeezing and stretching!

Mugly and Bugly are playing with play dough. They can make it change shape.

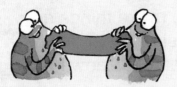

When they pull, the play dough **stretches**.

When they push, the play dough **squashes**.

I like to twist and bend the play dough. Some things will not stretch, squash, bend or twist.

shape can be changed

shape cannot be changed

Stretching is a pull. Squeezing is a push.

Workbook pages 38-39

Wizard's Practice

Write **Push** or **Pull** at the end of each sentence.

1. Pointy is kicking a ball. _____

2. I am lifting my teddy out of the box. _____

3. Wizard Whimstaff closes the drawer. _____

4. Mugly and Bugly are jumping. _____

5. Pointy opens the door. _____

Faster, faster

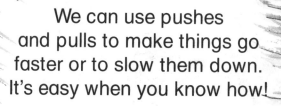

We can use pushes and pulls to make things go faster or to slow them down. It's easy when you know how!

Faster and slower.

Wizard Whimstaff and I go for a walk in the park. We watch the children going **faster**. They push harder to make things go faster.

Then we watched them trying to slow down. They are pulling hard to make things go **slower**. Super!

Pushing or pulling can make things speed up, slow down or change direction.

A fair test.

I want to test my toy car on a ramp.

I think that if I lift up one end of the ramp, the car will travel further. This is my **prediction**.

I let the car go from the same place each time.
I measure how far the car travels.
Then I make the ramp higher and let the car go again.
This is a fair test because I only change one thing and keep everything else the same. Super!
I only change the height of the ramp.

I keep these things the same: Starting place.
Ramp.
Car.

Here are my results. I have learnt that the higher the ramp, the farther the car will travel.

height of ramp	how far car travelled in cm
low	35
medium	80
high	130

Pushes and pulls are forces.

MAGIC WORDS faster • slower • prediction • fair test

Workbook pages 40-41

Wizard's Practice

Practice makes perfect. Write **F** for Faster or **S** for Slower next to each sentence.

1. Wizard Whimstaff pushes me harder on the swing. _____

2. Wizard Whimstaff hold the ropes on the swing. _____

3. Mugly holds onto Bugly's leg as he tries to swim away. _____

4. I push my car harder. _____

5. I pull back on the roundabout. _____

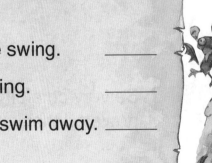

Exciting electricity

Now we are going to find out about how we use electricity, young wizard.

Electricity from the mains.

Our cave has mains **electricity**.

Allakazan! The electricity comes through the wires and the sockets. It gives us light and it works the television, the fridge, the cooker and the computer.

Lots of other things use mains electricity.

Electricity can be used to give us light.

Electricity can also give us sound.

Be very careful! The electricity that comes from the mains sockets is so powerful that it could hurt you. It is very dangerous.

 Never touch plugs with wet hands. The electricity could go through you and kill you.

Electricity from batteries.

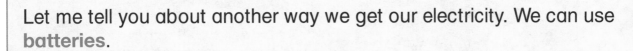

Let me tell you about another way we get our electricity. We can use **batteries**.

There are different size batteries for different things. My watch has a very small battery.

You have to put the batteries in the right way. They have **+** and **–** ends. Look at the pictures at the top of the page.

Batteries are not as powerful as mains electricity. They are much safer to use.

 Never cut open a battery, there are harmful chemicals inside.

 MAGIC WORDS electricity • batteries

Wizard's Practice

Workbook pages 42-43

Hey presto! Now finish these sentences by writing the missing words. Choose your words from this list.

> batteries   electricity   kill   sockets   wet

1 Mains electricity is very powerful and could _____ you.

2 Mains electricity comes through wires and _____ .

3 Never touch sockets with _____ hands.

4 Batteries provide _____ .

5 Our torch needs _____ .

Get connected

We have batteries, wires, bulbs and buzzers, so we can make lots of electrical circuits. Practice makes perfect!

Making circuits!

I connect the battery, wires and **bulb**. The **circuit** looks like this. The bulb lights up.

If I disconnect a wire, the bulb cannot light up. The electricity cannot flow around the wires, so the bulb cannot light.

All of the wires have to be connected so that the electricity can flow all the way around the circuit.

I can put a **buzzer** into the circuit. The buzzer makes a noise.

Faulty circuits.

Here is a circuit I made, but the bulb will not light because a wire is not connected. Can you see the fault?

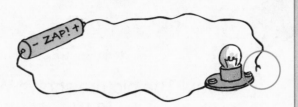

Miss Snufflebeam made these circuits. She has forgotten something in each circuit, so the bulbs will not light.

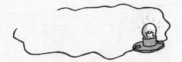  

Miss Snufflebeam has forgotten the battery.

Miss Snufflebeam has forgotten the bulb.

Miss Snufflebeam has forgotten the wire.

All of the wires and the parts have to be connected. Then the electricity can flow all around the circuit. Super!

Wizard's Practice

Workbook pages 44-45

It's easy when you know how! Write **T** for True or **F** for False at the end of each sentence.

1. All of the wires in the circuit need to be connected so that the bulb can light. _____

2. If a wire is not connected, the bulb will still light. _____

3. If a wire is not connected, the buzzer will not sound. _____

4. When wires and parts are all connected, electricity flows around the circuit. _____

5. The bulb will light without a battery. _____

Wizard's Challenge

 1 Circles of light.

Croak! The picture shows Wizard Whimstaff's cave. Can you circle the sources of light? We are off for a snooze!

 2 Naughty noises.

Burp! The pictures show things that make sound. Circle all the things that make a loud sound.

3 Pushing and pulling.

Croak! I pushed Bugly and he fell over. Pushes and pulls can make things move!

a Write push or pull under each picture.

_____   _____   _____   _____

Slurp! Here are some sentences about pushing and pulling. Write in the missing words.

> bend   push   squashed   stretched

b When we _____ down on a sponge, it gets squashed.

c A brick will not _____ easily.

d When we both push on our clay, it gets _____ .

e When we both pull on the rubber band, it gets _____ .

4 Circuits

Miss Snufflebeam is making electric circuits. The bulb lights up in only one of her circuits. Circle the circuit where the bulb will light.

Test Practice

1 a Label Pointy's body parts, using these words.

ear
finger
leg
head
arm

b Which of these body parts is used to hear? _____

c Which of these body parts is used to feel? _____

2 The pictures show different stages of life, but they are mixed up.

a Number each picture to show the correct order. The first one has been done for you.

  1

b The pictures show someone growing, feeding and moving. These are what all living things do. Write down something else that all living things do.

_____

3 Miss Snufflebeam lists the hair colour of all of the children in her class. Here is her list.

colour of hair	number of children
brown	12
blonde	8
black	4
red	1

Finish this bar chart for Miss Snufflebeam and then answer the questions.

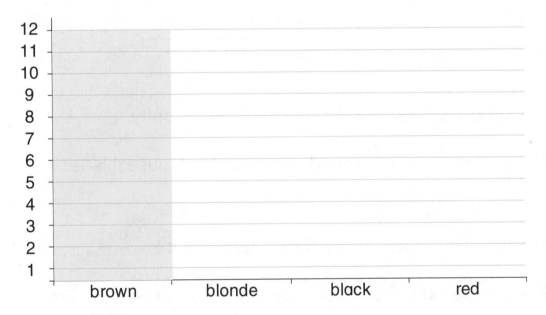

b Which colour hair did most children have?_____

c How many children had blonde hair?_____

d What colour hair did only one child have?_____

e How many children are in the class? _____

4 a Label the parts of this plant. Use these words.

stem

flower

leaf

roots

b Draw a line to match the part of the plant with the job that it does. The first one has been done for you.

holds the plant in the soil

makes food

takes water and goodness to all parts of the plant

attracts insects

5 Here are some properties of materials.

hard   transparent   soft

Finish the sentences by writing in the best property.

a The best material for a window is glass, because it is

_____ .

b The teddy is made from fur fabric, because it is _____ .

c The knife is made from metal, because it is _____ .

6 Match each object with its material. One is done for you.

wood   metal   plastic   paper   fabric

7 Some of these objects are natural and some have been made by people.

Circle the natural objects.

plastic doll   pebble   plant   pen   shell   polystyrene packaging

8 Pointy is making chocolate crispy cakes. Yum! He puts the chocolate in the pan and warms it up. Circle the correct word.

  a At the start, the chocolate is a ⎨ solid / liquid ⎬.

  b When he warms the chocolate, it turns into a ⎨ solid / liquid ⎬.

  c Pointy adds the crispies. The mixture is runny. He puts a spoonful of the mixture into each paper case. He leaves them in the fridge overnight. Describe what happens to the runny mixture.

_____

_____

9 Look at all the objects. Circle the objects that are a source of light.

10 Here are some sentences about sound. Finish the sentences by writing in the missing word. Use these words.

(loud)   (ears)   (quiet)   (waves)

   a We hear sounds with our_____ .

   b A fire engine makes a _____ noise.

   c Sound travels in _____ .

   d A mouse makes a _____ noise.

11 Here are some sentence beginnings and sentence endings, but they are mixed up.

Draw a line from each sentence beginning to its correct sentence ending.

   a To open the drawer, Pointy   it becomes squashed.

   b When you push play dough,   it stretches.

   c When you pull on a spring,   has to pull on the knob.

12 All of these things use electricity. Some use mains electricity and some use batteries.

   a Write **B** for battery or **M** for mains next to each picture.

_____   _____   _____   _____   _____   _____

Finish the sentences by writing in the missing word. Choose your words from this list.

| dangerous | dry | silly | wet |

b Mains electricity can be _____ .

c Never touch plugs or sockets with _____ hands.

13 Miss Snufflebeam has set up some electric circuits. Some of the bulbs will not light.

Put a tick ✔ next to the circuit where the bulb will light .

Put an ✗ next to the circuits where the bulb will not light.

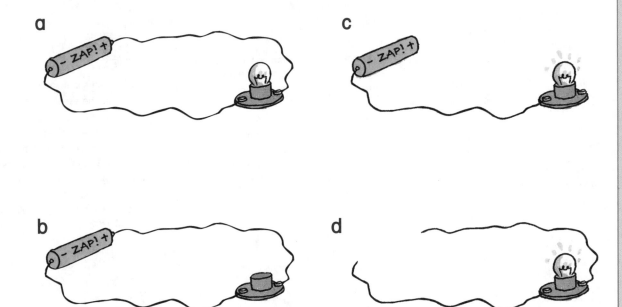

e When Miss Snufflebeam set up the above circuits, she forgot some things. Draw in the things she forgot in three of the pictures, so that each circuit will light up.

Answers

Page 5

1 smell
2 touch
3 see
4 taste
5 hear

Page 7

1 Unhealthy
2 Healthy
3 Unhealthy
4 Healthy
5 Unhealthy

Page 9

1 puppy — hen
2 chick — butterfly
3 caterpillar — dog
4 kitten — frog
5 tadpole — cat

Page 11

These answers are based on national averages, so may vary:
1 F
2 T
3 T
4 F
5 F

Page 13

1 exercise
2 hot
3 medicine
4 healthy
5 sweets

Page 14–15

Wizard's Challenge

1

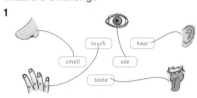

2 a

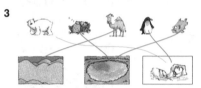

  b For a healthy **diet**, you should have a small amount from each food **group** and drink plenty of **water**.

3 b, c, e, d, a

4 a 10
  b 2
  c blue
  d green

Page 17

flower — attracts insects to visit the plant
leaf — where food is made for the plant
roots — carries food and water around the plant
roots — keep the plant in the soil
stem — suck up water from the soil

Page 19

1 water
2 sunlight
3 brown
4 yellow
5 leaves

Page 21

1 F
2 T
3 F
4 T
5 F

Page 23

1 flower
2 sprout
3 fruits
4 water
5 seeds

Page 25

non-living — tree
plant with thick trunk — sand
plant with flowers — slug
animal with no legs — cat
animal with legs — rose

Pages 26–27

Wizard's Challenge

1 a flower
  b roots
  c leaf
  d stem

2

3

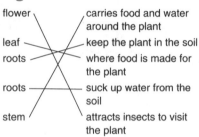

4 a Collect some soil in a pot. **1**
    Plant the seeds in the soil. **2**
    Place the pot in a warm place. **3**
    Water the seeds regularly. **4**
    (can accept 2 and 3 in reverse order)
  b We can get new plants from **seeds**.
  c When the seed is ready to **sprout**, the case splits open.
  d Then the new young plant can start to **grow**.

Page 29

1 shiny
2 transparent
3 flows
4 soft
5 hard

Page 31

1 T
2 F
3 T
4 T
5 F

Page 33

1 Y

2 Y

3 N

4 Y

5 Y

Page 34–35

Wizard's Challenge

1 a plastic
  b wood
  c glass
  d metal

2

3

4 a metals
  b magnetic
  c non-metals

5 a ice
  b water
  c steam

Page 37

1 R

2 S

3 S

4 R

5 S

Page 39

1 L

2 Q

3 L

4 L

5 Q

Page 41

1 ears

2 travels

3 danger

4 loud

5 quieter

Page 43

1 My house.

2 The train is travelling fast. ✔

3 The statue is very tall.

4 The children are playing football. ✔

5 The bus is coming. ✔

Page 45

1 push

2 pull

3 push

4 push

5 push or pull are both acceptable

Page 47

1 F

2 S

3 S

4 F

5 S

Page 49

1 kill

2 sockets

3 wet

4 electricity

5 batteries

Page 51

1 T

2 F

3 T

4 T

5 F

Pages 52–53

Wizard's Challenge

1

2

3 a

push   pull   push   pull

  b push
  c bend
  d squashed
  e stretched

4

Pages 54–61

Test Practice

1 a

head — finger
ear
arm
leg

b ear

c finger

2 a

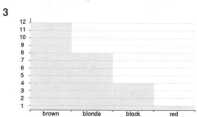

5   1   3   2   4

b Any one from: breathe, feel things, have babies, get rid of waste

3

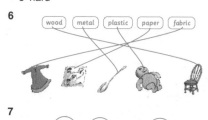

b brown

c 8

d red

e 25

4 a

flower
leaf
roots
stem

b

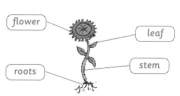

holds the plant in the soil
takes water and goodness to all parts of the plant
makes food
attracts insects

5 a transparent

b soft

c hard

6

wood   metal   plastic   paper   fabric

7

8 a solid

b liquid

c The mixture goes hard or turns into a solid.

9

10 a ears

b loud

c waves

d quiet

11 a To open the drawer, Pointy   it becomes squashed.

b When you push play dough,   it stretches.

c When you pull on a spring,   has to pull on the knob.

12 a

M   B   M   M   B   B

b dangerous

c wet

13 a ✔

b ✗

c ✗

d ✗

e Each circuit should look as follows:

- ZAP! +

Glossary

animals living things that are not plants

batteries chemicals react together inside a battery to provide us with electricity

bulb part of an electrical circuit that gives out light

buzzer part of an electrical circuit that gives out sound

circuit wires and parts connected together to allow electricity to flow

dark when there is no light, like at night-time

diet food that we eat

different when things are not the same

electricity a type of energy that can give us light, sound, heat and movement

exercise movements that strengthen your body

fair test only one factor is changed and all the rest are kept the same. This makes sure that you know what has caused your results

faster when things speed up

flower part of a plant that attracts insects

freezes when water cools down and turns into ice

fruits part of a plant that contains seeds

gas a material that fills the container it is in and does not keep its shape

grow when living things become bigger

healthy when you are healthy, you are fit and feeling well

hear one of our senses using the ears

heavier when you measure your weight, you are measuring how heavy you are. Some people are heavier than others

height a measure of how tall you are

high a scream is a high sound

humans living things, grouped as part of the animal kingdom

investigating series of experiments to answer a question

leaf green part of a plant where food is made

light source something that gives out light

liquid a material that can flow and takes the shape of its container

listen you use your ears to listen to sounds

living when things can move, have babies, feel things, grow, breathe, get rid of waste and feed, they are living

loud a noisy sound, like the sound made by a car horn

low a growl is a low sound

magnetic some metals that are attracted towards north

manufactured things made by people

materials what everything is made from

medicine pills and liquids given by your doctor to make you feel better

melts when a solid heats up and turns into a liquid

move when things go from one place to another

natural materials materials found in nature, not made by a person

noise unwanted sound

non-living things that cannot carry out all of the activities of moving, having babies, feeling, growing, breathing, getting rid of waste and feeding are non-living

plants living things that use sunlight to make their own food from air and water

prediction what you think will happen

properties things that describe different materials, such as soft and warm

pull a pull is a type of force

push a push is a type of force

quiet a soft sound, like the sound made by a mouse

reflects to bounce light off a surface

roots the part of a plant that anchors it into the soil and takes in water

see we see things with our eyes, this is one of our senses

seeds the part of a plant that will sprout to make a new plant

similar when things are nearly the same

shiny reflects light

slower when things slow down

smell we smell things with our nose, this is one of our senses

solid a rigid material that keeps its shape

sprout when a seed first starts to grow into a plant

squash to push a material together

stem where water and food are moved around a plant

stretch to pull a material apart

sunlight light from the sun

taller when you measure your height, you are measuring how tall you are. Some people are taller than others

taste when we eat our food, we can taste it with our tongue. This is one of our senses

touch when we touch things, we can feel them with our skin. This is one of our senses

unhealthy unhealthy people are unfit or ill

water rain falls as water, which fills our rivers and lakes